This Book Belongs To

_____

Gifted By

_____

You Were Meant to Fly

You Were Meant To Fly

Written by Natalie Greene

COPYRIGHT

Unless otherwise noted, all Scriptures are taken from the King James Version of the Bible.

Book Title: You Were Meant to Fly
Copyright © Author Natalie Greene
Print ISBN: 978-1-944566-70-8

Published by Bush Publishing & Associates
BushPublishing.com
Tulsa, Oklahoma

Contents and/or cover may not be reproduced in whole or in part in any form without the express written consent of the author. All rights are reserved under International Copyright Law.
Printed in the United States.

Dedication

To my beautiful children. May you always dream big, trust in God's plan, and know that all things are possible with God. Keep believing in yourselves as I believe in you. You are my greatest blessings, and I am forever grateful to be your guide on this journey of life.

On a crisp fall night

with the harvest moon very bright,

one egg by mistake

took a long fall...

Across the river bend,

down to the bank,

rolled the egg in a fenced pen,

and it sank.

The sun came up

and the sun came down

on the little speckled egg

with the cooped-up chickens

all around.

Time went by the chickens

clucking away...

But something was different

about the egg this day.

With the warmth of the sun,

the egg began breaking.

For all this time

there was a miracle in the making.

Out "burst" new life

in the coop that day.

And to everyone's surprise,

this little chicken was

much bigger in size.

The little bird grew

and learned how to roam

like a chicken.

Even though deep down

he knew

he was different.

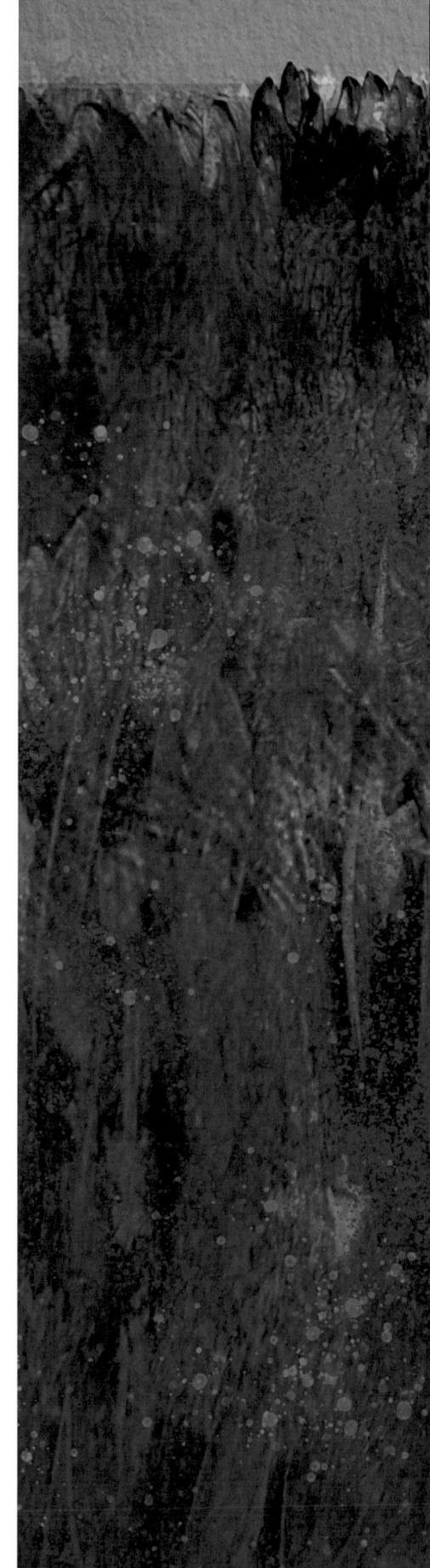

The little chicken noticed,

out of the corner of his eye-

he saw the eagles flying,

high in the sky.

Watching the eagles is how

he would spend his days,

but he kept clucking away because

that's what a prairie chicken does.

Little did he know,

to soar with the eagles

is who he truly was.

Knowing in his heart

he wasn't the same...

The bird kept on seeking

but the answers never came.

Until one day the biggest

of all the eagles came down,

to save the little bird

where he was no longer bound.

"You're not meant to soar,

you're not meant to fly,

your home is in the dirt

not in the sky"

"I've noticed you looking,

you want to fly just like me.

You are brave, you are special,

take my wing and you'll see.

Up and away

they rose to new heights,

the little bird flapped

with all of his might.

At this moment

the bird's destiny was born...

he realized. I'm an eagle!

And he no longer felt torn.

He was happy, he was free,

flying high in the sky

he thought, I knew it was in me.

In the sky to new heights

on my way let it be!

The End

Just like the little bird who was destined to fly, God has made you so very special. There is greatness in you. You have a destiny, passion, and divine purpose. So every time you look up to the sky know without a doubt in your heart that you were made for something BIG! You are unique, you are special, you're as bright as a beam. Don't ever give up, and always follow your dreams!

About the Author

Natalie is a passionate writer with a heart devoted to inspiring others to dream beyond their limits and trust in the power of faith in God. Through her heartfelt words, she encourages her readers to embrace their God-given potential and pursue their greatest aspirations with courage and conviction. Drawing from her own experiences of overcoming challenges, Natalie believes that when we align our dreams with God's purpose, anything is possible. Her books offer a message of hope, empowerment, and unwavering faith, reminding readers that they are never alone in their journey to dream big and live boldly.

www.ingramcontent.com/pod-product-compliance
Lightning Source LLC
Chambersburg PA
CBRC091726070526
44586CB00008B/88